Storytelling Basics:
How To Get Started In Telling
Impactful Stories

*Part one of **The Storytelling Mastery**: How To Elevate Your Business and Build Personal Influence with The Power Of Storytelling*

Last updated - December 2023

Obehi Ewanfoh

ISBN: 9798376952726
ISBN: 9798377021674
info@obehiewanfoh.com
Obehiewanfoh.com

What I have learned from over 10 years of storytelling experience, 2013 to 2023

Table of Contents

DEDICATION

This book is a heartfelt tribute to those individuals whose unwavering support guided me through the intricate immigration processes in Italy.

As I embarked on my research, delving into the presence of Africans in northern Italy (The Journey), I did so with limited knowledge of the challenges that lay ahead. I will talk a little more about the details of how it all began later in this book.

The invaluable assistance I received from these individuals not only illuminated my path but also served as a constant source of inspiration, shaping the work I pursue today.

I express my deepest gratitude to each of them, and it is with immense joy that I dedicate this first book in the **Storytelling Mastery** to those remarkable individuals.

IMPORTANT:

This book series is designed for those looking to elevate their businesses and build personal influence with the power of storytelling.

This is not just another book about storytelling. This is a **Full Package** to help you start from the ABC of storytelling to some of the most advanced strategies of leveraging the power of story in your business.

Start your 7 days free access to our Storytelling Mastery **Academy.AClasses.org**

INTRODUCTION

There is huge power in storytelling and knowing how to correctly tell your story can set you apart from the noise out there. Trust me on that.

Would you rather join our community of business owners and professional individuals who are continually improving themselves in storytelling for business? Then check out AClasses Academy. It's available at Aclasses.org.

The following is a clip about the power of storytelling from Chimamanda Ngozi Adichie, the famous Nigerian writer with multiple awards, including the Women's Prize for Fiction, PEN Open Book Award, and much more:

> *"Stories have been used to dispossess and to malign. But stories can also be used to empower and to humanize. Stories can break the dignity of a people.*

But stories can also repair that broken dignity."[1]

Such is the awesome power of storytelling, and it's highly relevant across all industries, irrespective of what you do and where you might be operating. If you are in the business of dealing with human beings, then you need to learn how to leverage the power of storytelling.

When it comes to business, you need to understand that today, the world of branding and marketing is a constantly changing landscape. To make an impact and get noticed as a small business, you must be able to tell compelling stories that can resonate with your target audience. Stories are what make brands memorable, relationships personal, and experiences authentic.

The following is a clip about the effectiveness of brand storytelling and it's available at Thebrandshopbw.com:

"55% of consumers are more likely to remember a story than a list of facts. 68%

---

[1] *Chimamanda Ngozi Adichie – A Nigerian writer.*

of consumers say that brand stories influence their purchasing decisions. Companies with compelling brand stories have a 20% increase in customer loyalty. 64% of consumers make a purchase after watching a branded social media video." [2]

Going further, the article, written by Tumisang Bogwasi added, citing the Harvard Business Review that human brains are naturally attuned to storytelling and tend to respond better to narratives than to other forms of content sharing. That is an article you should consider reading and if have been attending our weekly LinkedIn audio live events on storytelling where we bring in different experts to speak on the question of storytelling, you would understand how much importance we place this. Trust me, the game of marketing and business in general has changed but storytelling can help you ride to success if well executed.

Seth Godin is an entrepreneur with one of the most popular blogs in the world. He is also a speaker and best-selling author with over 20 best-

---

[2] *Brand Storytelling in 2023: The Latest Statistics and Trends - Thebrandshopbw.com.*

selling books. Here is how he summed up the argument in one line.

> *"Marketing is no longer about the stuff that you make, but about the stories you tell."*[3]

I want you to take a moment to think about that and imagine what you can do with your ability to tell great and impactful stories. Consider your content creation process, the marketing needs for your small business, and what the power of storytelling can do for your entrepreneurial journey. That is what is fueling this conversation and several others that will follow.

Sure, storytelling is an essential skill for marketers, entrepreneurs, and business owners who want to stand out from the competition. To create an unforgettable brand, or better connect with the African diaspora community, you need to understand how to craft a story that will resonate with your audience.

There cannot be two ways about that. And that is true whether you are talking of fortune 500

---

[3] *Seth Godin - an American author and former dot com business executive.*

companies in New York City or a roadside businesswoman in your neighborhood. This is what I am here to help you understand.

Welcome to **The Storytelling Mastery**: How To Elevate Your Business and Build Personal Influence with The Power Of Storytelling.

This book is created with beginners in mind, and it covers all you need to know even if you are new to storytelling. By the end of the book, you should be able to create effective stories for your business so you can better connect with your audience and earn more from what you do. The book series will teach you from the basic setup of a story, all the way up including:

- How to develop your storytelling skills,
- How to target your audience and connect at an emotional level,
- And how to profit from the stories you tell.

How the book series is set up

It was in the early period of 2013 that I first started to collect data about the African diaspora community and then, it was mainly those in northern Italy through a series of interviews. It was an interesting encounter with the direct protagonists, many of whom have now relocated to different parts of the world in their immigration journey. Yes, some have equally relocated to their home countries in Africa.

I have already published two books from the research project, (*The Journey: Africans In Verona* and *The color Of Our Children*), now, 10 years later, I still love what I have done, documenting the experiences of the people so that those who will be here later can benefit or learn something from their experiences. Feeling that some other people might also be interested in learning how to tap into the power of storytelling, I have decided to share what I have learned over these years.

But would you say it is important for more people to learn about storytelling today? Well, I leave you to reflect on that.

The work, drawn from my research experience of working with different people over the years, it's voluminous, and knowing the feeling of some people towards reading in the African diaspora community, I have decided to break up the work into manageable chunks for easier consumption. That is how the book became a five-part series, each volume treating a different part of the argument.

Your storytelling guides

The storytelling guides are designed to help you get more out of this reading. Each chapter of the book starts with a premise of what you can get by the end of the reading. That is followed by diving into the specific topic, citing instances, and elaborating on the chosen argument for further clarification.

Towards the end of each chapter are "your storytelling guides", a set of actionable recommendations on how to leverage what was discussed in the specific chapter. If you pay attention to this section of the book, you will have a lot to benefit from it as designed.

Your chapter takeaways

Let me be clear that this book is not just to be read for the pure purpose of occupying your time. There is a clear thought behind every chapter that is included in this book series, otherwise, that chapter should not have been there. So, from each chapter, there are key takeaways for you.

Just after the "storytelling guides", you will see some highlights which are in line with the initial premise at the beginning of the specific chapter. This is to be sure that you get the true value for which that chapter of the book was written. That is not by accident, so pay attention.

Before we jump to chapter one of the book, let me share a personal experience with you. Sure, I was born, and grew up in Nigeria, but I am currently in Italy as I write this book. Storytelling has always remained part of what I do for as far back as I can remember.

I am the host of the Obehi Podcast; I create online training courses and I am extremely passionate about the power of storytelling. Apart from the business storytelling section where we teach small business owners how to leverage the power of storytelling in their business communication, I also have a video storytelling series, "Life and Legacy", where we talk about prominent people of African descent, both in Africa and in the diaspora.

To learn more about my motivation for writing this book and more, please check out the last part of this book.

CHAPTER 1: BEGINNERS' TIPS FOR STORYTELLING

Storytelling is like a tool belt for small business owners. By that I mean stories are the key to crafting content that truly resonates with your audience, builds trust, and ultimately drives sales. But for beginners, mastering the art of storytelling can be like starting a new construction project without any tools in your belt.

If that is how it appears to you, don't worry. With the help of some useful guides and practical tips, you can fill your tool belt with everything you need to unlock your storytelling potential. So, get ready to unleash your creativity and take your storytelling to the next level. If you pay attention to the end, you will be just like a carpenter who has all the right tools to build a beautiful home.

Soon, you will realize that with each new story you create, you are adding another tool to your belt, thereby strengthening your storytelling skills, and bringing your brand to life.

Sounds interesting? Now let's get started.

Understanding the basics of storytelling

Welcome to the first chapter of Storytelling Basics: How To Get Started In Telling Impactful Stories. In this first chapter of the book, we will consider the basics you need to know about storytelling and there is a reason for this as you will soon understand.

By the end of this chapter, you should understand what is meant by storytelling, and what is the meaning of a story. You need to understand these basics of storytelling and how to correctly apply them in your small business and content creation strategy.

Now, I want you to imagine yourself in a house one afternoon and you receive a call that in a few days, the company you are working for will be closing their operation in your city and if you want to keep working for them, you need to come to another city where they might have an opportunity for you.

Will you not consider asking yourself some questions, like:

- Transportation,
- The possibility of relocating to the new city,
- Are you going to get the same kind of job there?
- Or is it simply better to look for another job in your current location?

Those are the basics, and no one does anything serious without first considering the basics.

About 60 years ago today, the US President, John F. Kennedy delivered an address at Rice University. In that address, titled: "We Choose the Moon", he inspired Americans to support NASA's mission to the moon. That was when President John F. Kennedy promised to put an American astronaut on the moon before the end of the 1960s.

Now, don't you think President John F. Kennedy and NASA's "The National Aeronautics and Space Administration" needed to consider the basics for their mission to the moon?

Yes, they did, and that is what we are equally going to do in this first book of "**The Storytelling**

Mastery: How To Elevate Your Business and Build Personal Influence with The Power Of Storytelling".

Now, let's get started with the first and obvious question: "What is storytelling?" This is a beginner's question, and the answer is right here below.

What is storytelling?

Storytelling is the art and process of using words, images, sounds, or other forms of communication to convey a narrative or a series of events to an audience. It is a fundamental aspect of human culture and has been used for millennia to entertain, inform, educate, and inspire.

Yes, storytelling can also be used by content creators as a marketing tool. And small businesses, looking at their necessity to better connect with their audience, must learn how to tap into the power of storytelling.

On April 4, 2019, Will Storr, a British former photographer, and journalist released the book: Science Of Storytelling and the book has well over 1,629 ratings on Amazon.

In the book, Storr provided valuable guides for animate readers and at the same time helped writers shape their narratives. Here is my favorite quote from the book:

"Locked inside the black vault of our skulls, stuck forever in the solitude of our own hallucinated universe, story is a portal, a hallucination within the hallucination, the closest we'll ever really come to escape."[4]

Consider reflecting on that and if possible, read the entire book because there is a lot to gain from it. Understanding the deep psychological impulses of novels, Storr uses neuroscience and psychotherapy to demonstrate why the novel, or if you like storytelling in general has become so important in our cultural lives. We will talk about the science of storytelling in the second chapter of this book. So, look out for that.

Every culture has its own stories and narratives which are shared as a means of entertainment, educational literacy, and pure fun!

I was born in Uromi, Nigeria. I remember growing up as a child in our village of Amedokhian. I was always fascinated to go out every evening and listen to stories. I am talking about over 40 years ago and today in 2023, such is almost impossible

---

[4] *Science Of Storytelling by Will Storr.*

to come by in Uromi. The way we share our stories has changed but the stories themselves and what they represent have not changed.

My son, for example, was born here in Italy. Growing up, he had access to video games and cartoons on television, computer, and smartphone but he still craves storytelling a great deal. In fact, at one point my son would not sleep until I had told him a story at night.

How does the power of storytelling skill effectively shape the narrative of a person? Make sure to remember that question because it will become relevant later in the book series when we cite the incident of Nelson Mandela and the campaign against the apartheid regime in South Africa. We will come to that later.

As for the previous instance, I spent a lot of time, talking about it in one of my books: "Amende - The Stream Water", a 2015 short story that explored the delicate balance of African society and the difference between human and divine justice systems.

Stories have always played an important role in our lives and will continue to do so in the foreseeable future. Now, I want you to pay attention to a short piece from one of the most popular books in Africa.

> "A man who calls his kinsmen to a feast does not do so to save them from starving.

They all have food in their own homes. When we gather together in the moonlit village ground it is not because of the moon. Every man can see it in his own compound. We come together because it is good for kinsmen to do so."[5]

That is from the book, Things Fall Apart by the late Nigerian writer, Dr. Chinua Achebe. And I want to believe you have gotten the sense of that piece.

You see, every one of us has read and listened to different stories at one time or the other. This is whether we are talking about the life of great people like the black French revolutionary, Thomas Alexandre Dumas, the great American Fredrick Douglas of the 19th century, and the organizers of the Black Lives Matter Movement which started on July 13, 2013, we are always reading about stories and those stories continue to shape our own lives.

Here, however, we are not only talking about consuming stories but creating an experience for the audience. How do you feel about being a

---

[5] *Things Fall Apart by Dr. Chinua Achebe.*

storyteller and creating an experience for your audience? You truly need to reflect on that.

As a storyteller, your audience will want to know the protagonist, their struggle, and how they overcome their challenges. They will need the context of what led up to the climax and then they will want to know how things eventually wrapped up like in the historic events I mentioned above. All of that is storytelling and they are what make our lives and shape our societies into what they are today.

Talking about your audience, I want you to think about how Dale Carnegie, put it.

> "Your purpose is to make your audience see what you saw, hear what you heard, feel what you felt. Relevant detail, couched in concrete, colorful language, is the best way to recreate the incident as it happened and to picture it for the audience."[6]

---

[6] Dale Carnegie was an American writer and lecturer, and the developer of courses in self-improvement,

It's absolutely important that when you are crafting your content, you think about who your audience is, and what their common motivations and goals are so you can better connect with them.

You will hear me repeat the theme of the audience throughout this five-part book series and if you ever come to our weekend LinkedIn audio event on storytelling mastery, you will hear me say the say too.

That is because the choice of audience and its perfect understanding is indispensable to the success or failure of our storytelling. As a minimum, you need to ask yourself the following three questions:

1. What problems are they trying to solve?
2. How do they feel when they encounter these problems?
3. What are their hopes and fears?

Knowing your audience will help you create an authentic experience that will work for them. We

---

salesmanship, corporate training, public speaking, and interpersonal skills." – Wikipedia.com.

will talk more about these in another book in the series when we consider content and audience research for better engagement. Look out for that.

Having talked about storytelling, it's time to look at the "story" itself. What is the meaning of a story?

What is the meaning of a story?

This is a good question to reflect on. Well, a story is a description of an event in a sequence of words and sentences. It can be about something that has happened in the past or something that might happen in the future but is presented in a logical sense and can trigger an emotion in the audience.

The history of storytelling goes back several thousands of years, both in oral narration and graphic representation of events and experiences.

Long before some of the first humans migrated out of Africa, our ancestors were able to travel the large continent because they kept an accurate record of their movement. They knew such vital information as:

- Places of food,
- Where to get water,

- And of course, where the danger lies to avoid.

Without this essential information, they would not have survived and consequently, we would not have been here today. So, storytelling is also about our survival, not just for entertainment purposes. I am telling you this so that you can treat storytelling with the utmost attention and seriousness it deserves. Also, later in the series when we shall be talking about connecting with your audience and leveraging storytelling for great results in business, you will know where we are coming from.

Some of the earliest representations in storytelling date back as far as 30,000 years ago. The first stories were animal fables[7], which depicted animals and humans interacting with each other. Some of these texts were carved into

---

[7] "In literature, a fable (pronounced fey-buh l) is a short fictional story that has a moral or teaches a lesson. Fables use humanized animals, objects, or parts of nature as main characters, and are therefore considered to be a sub-genre of fantasy." - What is a Fable? - Literaryterms.net.

caves and stone tablets and are still preserved today.

And of course, before our ancestors ever learned to cave and paint into stones, they had been sharing stories of all kinds, including oral narration. Oral narration is one of the most ancient forms of storytelling and a great method of human communication. Even to date, it's still highly relevant and probably will never be replaced in the near future.

While, today, our storytelling might have evolved so much, with all the technology and gadgets at our disposal, the art of storytelling has remained almost the same. It has remained the craving and irresistible element in human conversation and that is a huge power in the hands of the storyteller. But do you really understand how powerful you are as a storyteller? That is a question you need to reflect on.

I like the way Ben Okri puts it. Born in Minna, the capital city of Niger State, Nigeria, Ben Okri OBE is a Nigerian-British poet and novelist. His writing is considered to be emblematic of post-colonial literary traditions, and he has often been compared to other prominent authors, including Salman Rushdie (an Indian-born British-American novelist) and Gabriel García (the popular Colombian novelist).

This is how Ben reflected on the power and the responsibility of storytellers:

"To poison a nation, poison its stories. A demoralized nation tells demoralized stories to itself. Beware of the storytellers who are not fully conscious of the importance of their gifts, and who are irresponsible in the application of their art."[8]

As storytellers, we must be conscious of the power we have because "the mystery of storytelling", said Ben Okri is the miracle of a single living seed that can populate several acres of human minds.

Storytelling is a powerful instrument, and every real story must have a beginning, middle, and end. It should also have characters, a setting, and a plot. We will talk more about each of these later in the book series.

A good story, as I have already pointed out, should have a compelling protagonist and antagonist with a conflict between them. These are the instruments to tell a great story and a great

---

[8] *Ben Okri - A Nigerian-British poet and a novelist.*

story is one that the audience hardly forgets. Always keep that at the back of your mind.

The relevance of storytelling for small businesses

Storytelling can be a powerful tool for small businesses in various ways. In the words of Chris Brogan, Author, Marketing Consultant, Journalist, and Speaker, "Stories are how we learn best. We absorb numbers and facts and details, but we keep them all glued into our heads with stories."

Now, here are five key reasons why storytelling is relevant for small businesses and why as a small business owner you need to pay more attention to the basics of storytelling:

1. **Building a Brand Identity:** Small businesses often struggle to differentiate themselves in a crowded marketplace. Storytelling allows them to create a unique brand identity by sharing their history, values, and mission. Customers are more likely to connect with a brand that has a compelling story, making it easier for the business to stand out and build a loyal customer base. Did that sound like what you want for your business or professional life?

2. **Creating Emotional Connections:** Stories can evoke emotions, and emotional connections are essential for

customer loyalty. Sharing stories about the challenges you have overcome, the people behind the business, or the impact you have had on customers' lives can all help create a deep emotional bond between your brand and your audience.

3. **Communicating Values and Mission:** All small businesses need to have strong values and a clear mission. Storytelling provides a platform to effectively communicate these principles. When customers understand what a business stands for and believes in, they are more likely to align themselves with that business and become advocates.

4. **Humanizing the Brand:** Stories put a human face on a business. Sharing anecdotes about the founders, employees, or even customers can humanize your brand, making it more relatable and approachable. Never forget that people want to connect with real individuals and their experiences, and storytelling allows you to showcase the human side of your business.

5. **Educating and Informing:** Storytelling can be a powerful tool for educating your audience about your products or services. Instead of presenting dry facts and features, you can use stories to illustrate how your offerings solve real problems or enhance customers' lives. This approach is more engaging and memorable, thereby

making it easier for customers to understand the value you provide.

In summary, storytelling is a valuable strategy for small businesses because it helps build a unique brand identity, fosters emotional connections, communicates values and mission, humanizes the brand, and educates and informs customers more engagingly.

These elements can ultimately lead to increased customer loyalty, brand recognition, and business growth.

Storytelling guide - Beginners' tips for storytelling

Here are some beginner's guides to storytelling. Make sure to pay attention to each of them and see how they can apply to your specific case:

1. **Know your audience**: Identifying and understanding the values, beliefs, and desires of your target audience can help guide the story you tell and make it more relatable to them.
2. **Have a clear structure**: A well-structured story has a clear beginning, middle, and end. We will talk more about story structure in a later chapter of this book. However, make sure your story follows a logical

progression so you can keep the audience engaged.

3. **The "show, don't tell"**: Instead of simply describing events, bring them to life with clear descriptions and sensory details to make the story more engaging.

4. **Use vivid and emotional language**: In your stories, consider using words that evoke emotions, paint pictures, and transport your audience into the story world.

5. **Make it personal**: Adding some personal anecdotes, experiences or perspectives can make your story more relatable, memorable, and impactful. This also sets your story apart from others in the same industry or genre.

Your takeaway from chapter one

What is your takeaway? Well, remember the key points that we discussed in this chapter. Storytelling involves weaving together characters, events, and themes to create a narrative that engages and captivates the listener or reader. It can take many forms, including oral narration, written stories, movies, comics, and much more.

The goal of storytelling is to connect with the audience and communicate ideas, emotions, and values in a memorable and impactful way.

This first chapter of the book shows you what you need to do to get your foot at the door. It helped you understand what storytelling is and what is meant by the term "story".

See you in the next chapter where we shall talk about "The Science Of Storytelling". That too, is an important conversation. So, get ready for it.

CHAPTER 2: THE SCIENCE OF STORYTELLING

Intuitively, we can tell when we are engaged in a good story. But recent research is shedding light on why storytelling has such a profound impact on us.

As it turns out, experiencing a story can trigger changes in our neurochemical processes, making stories a powerful force in shaping human behavior. All these explain that there is more to the power of storytelling than often discussed in some random places.

Stories are not only tools for connection and entertainment but can also be used to influence and exert control. This is the science of storytelling, and you will be doing yourself and your business a great favor by understanding it.

Welcome to chapter 2 of the book, Storytelling Basics: How To Get Started In Telling Impactful Stories. In this second chapter of the book, we will talk about the science of storytelling, why small businesses need to start tapping into the power of storytelling and what is the difference between stories and narratives.

Is there a science to storytelling?

Yes, there is science behind storytelling and it's the study of how stories are constructed and how they affect people, both personally and in their professional lives. When we engage in a good narrative, we ignite emotions within the audience.

The receptors in our brains react to the words we come across, either pulling us further into the story or prompting us to approach it with caution.

This phenomenon encapsulates both the art and the science of storytelling, and becoming proficient in it is a valuable talent for eliciting emotions through stories.

> *"Locked inside the black vault of our skulls, stuck forever in the solitude of our own hallucinated universe, story is a portal, a hallucination within the*

hallucination, the closest we'll ever really come to escape."[9]

– from The Science of Storytelling by Will Storr.

The science of storytelling includes how we analyze the elements of a story, such as character, plot, and theme, and how they work together to create meaning and elicit emotional responses in the audience.

It also involves studying the psychological and neurological effects of stories on the brain, and how people use stories to make sense of their own lives and the world around them.

In a publication written by Lani Peterson and Vanessa Boris, Senior Manager, Video Solutions at Harvard Business Publishing Corporate Learning, they urge organizations to build a strong storytelling culture and inculcate storytelling at the heart of their learning programs. And there are valid reasons behind that recommendation.

---

[9] *The Science of Storytelling - Will Storr*

"Storytelling," started the publication, The Science Behind The Art Of Storytelling, has the power to engage, influence, teach, and inspire listeners. So, you surely need to build storytelling into your content creation and communication strategy.

This is particularly important for you if you own a small business and you truly want to connect with your audience at an emotional level. And of course, the use of storytelling for business is not less important even if you are a big multinational or fortune 500 company.

> *"There's an art to telling a good story, and we all know a good story when we hear one. But there's also a science behind the art of storytelling."[10]*

"It is easy", said Fredrick Lui Adama, "to get swept into all the brain hype. News articles splash

_____

[10] *The Science Behind The Art Of Storytelling - Harvardbusiness.org.*

headlines about how brain images show that reading Jane Austen makes you smarter."[11]

In his work, "The Science of Storytelling: Perspectives from Cognitive Science, Neuroscience, and the Humanities", Fredrick stated that emotion is a defining ingredient in narrative fiction. And if we don't experience the emotion then we are probably less involved in the story. The lack of emotion can make us attend less to the story or reject it altogether.

The science of storytelling can be used in such fields as psychology, marketing, and education, all to better understand how to effectively communicate ideas and engage people through storytelling. There, surely, are a lot of benefits to storytelling and as for the use of stories in marketing, we will consider that later in this book series. So, look out for that.

Now here are 5 science-based benefits of storytelling to get you thinking:

---

[11] *The Science of Storytelling: Perspectives from Cognitive Science, Neuroscience, and the Humanities - Fredrick Lui Adama.*

1. **Improving memory**: Studies have shown that hearing and telling stories can improve our memory and retention, especially when the story is emotionally charged.
2. **Promoting empathy**: Stories can help people understand and relate to others by providing insight into their experiences and emotions.
3. **Enhancing social bonds**: Sharing stories with others can help create a sense of connection and build stronger relationships in the process.
4. **Facilitating learning**: Another great benefit of stories is around teaching and learning, as they can help make complex concepts more relatable and easier to understand.
5. **Reducing stress**: Listening to stories, particularly ones with positive themes, can help reduce stress and promote relaxation in the audience.

The science of storytelling refers to the study of how stories affect human behavior and cognition. It involves understanding the psychological and neurobiological mechanisms that underlie the power of storytelling, all to influence our thoughts, our feelings, and our actions.

It is based on this understanding that storytelling is continuously been used in all marketing, sales, and communication agencies, like no other tool. It's also for this reason that we encourage small businesses and content creators to tap more into the power of storytelling.

For example, a recent study found that when people hear a story, their brains respond as if they were experiencing the events of the story themselves. This is known as "neural coupling" and it is thought to be one of the reasons why stories are so powerful in influencing our emotions and behavior.

In the article, Why Storytelling Works, the writer, talking about why stories can grab the attention of people from their bubbles, said: "The human brain has a strong tendency to lose focus." And that "it is estimated to engage in up to 2,000 daydreams a day and to spend up to half its waking time wandering."

This goes to show, according to the writer, that storytelling is a highly effective way to communicate information, establish connections, and market products and concepts. It equally helps to motivate others like no other means of communication and information sharing. So, you need to tap more into the power of storytelling for your own good.

> "When the brain sees or hears a story, its neurons fire in the same patterns as the speaker's brain... "Mirror neurons" create coherence between a speaker's brain and

the brains of his/her audience members."[12]

Another example of the science of storytelling is the way it can be used to change people's attitudes and beliefs. It has been found that people who read a fictional story that portrayed a character overcoming a stereotype were more likely to have a positive attitude toward the group the character belonged to.

Moreover, storytelling can also be used to help people remember information better. A study published in "Cognitive Science" found that people were more likely to remember information presented in the form of a story than in the form of a list of facts.

Cognitive science combines insights from various fields like linguistics, neuroscience, anthropology, and computer science to explore the workings of the human mind. It investigates how different tasks and functions affect our cognitive processes.

---

[12] *Why Storytelling Works: The Science - Arielgroup.com*

Understanding the potential of cognitive science and neuroscience, you can perfectly use stories to make a powerful connection and persuade people, either for personal reasons or business purposes. It can also help you unveil the immense power of narrative and leverage the influence it has on our brains.

Talking of the human brain and the power of narratives, collective or individual, there is probably nothing else that has attracted more attention in all human history. This is whether you are examining ancient African civilizations and the modern world where we now have more tools to examine our behavior and interactions as species.

The following is a clip from the article, How Stories Connect and Persuade Us - Unleashing the Brain Power of Narrative:

> "We all know this delicious feeling of being swept into a story world. You forget about

your surroundings, and you are entirely immersed. "[13]

As said by Uri Hasson, professor of psychology and neuroscience at Princeton University, your brain waves start to synchronize with those of the storyteller as you hear a story unfold. This is probably why no human culture has ever outgrown the power of storytelling. It's deeply rooted in all of us.

With his research team where they recorded the brain activity between a storyteller and an audience, Professor Uri found that the greater the listener's comprehension, the more closely the brain wave patterns of the listener mirrored those of the storyteller. It's like "I am trying to make your brain similar to mine in areas that capture the meaning, the situation, the schema — the context of the world", he added.

As stated earlier, the science of storytelling is a complex field that explores how stories influence our thoughts, feelings, and behavior. Studies have shown that stories can create neural

---

[13] *How Stories Connect And Persuade Us: Unleashing The Brain Power Of Narrative - Npr.org*

coupling, change attitudes and beliefs, and aid in memory retention.

Are you still wondering why storytelling is deeply rooted in such fields as psychology, spirituality, deep intelligent gathering and investigation, marketing, military, and practically all aspects of human conduct? This is literally how we function and it's not any kind of speculation.

In one publication by Labster, a leading platform for virtual labs and science simulations, the writer stated that "Storytelling in science can be used to bridge the gap between theory and reality, by focusing the subject on why students are learning what they are learning."[14]

Now, stop and reflect on that for a moment. What if like the student, you can flip it around for your audience and customers? If you think about it, that is what we are talking about here in this book. If you truly understand the basics of storytelling and how it works, you can effectively deploy it in

_____

[14] *How can science teachers use storytelling? (Part 2) - Labster.com*

your content creation and marketing strategy for your small business.

That is an immersed power in your hands, and anybody can leverage it. You can start from where you are.

We can all benefit from storytelling

Storytelling is a tool that can be used by everyone to communicate and connect with others. It is a universal language that transcends cultural, language, and age barriers. This is because stories are based on human experiences and emotions, which are easily relatable and accessible to everyone.

Stories have been used for thousands of years to pass down knowledge, traditions, and values from one generation to the next. They have the power to engage, educate, and entertain, making them an effective way to communicate complex ideas and messages to people.

In his famous TED Talk, "The Clues to a Great Story," Andrew Stanton, a celebrated writer, and director at Pixar Animation Studios shares his insights into the elements that make a story great. He argues that a great story has three key components:

1. Emotion,
2. Theme,

3. And character.

Emotion is what makes a story relatable, as it connects the audience to the story on a deeper level. The theme is the central idea that the story is exploring and what the audience will take away from the story. Character is what drives the story forward and it's what makes the audience care about the story.

Stanton emphasizes that a great story should evoke an emotional response, communicate a universal truth, and be driven by well-rounded and compelling characters. He also shares tips for writers on how to create memorable stories that will resonate with their audiences.

All these tips are continuously elaborated upon with case studies and personal examples with different experts on our weekly audio live event on LinkedIn. You might consider checking us out to learn more.

In today's world, technology has made storytelling even more accessible. There are now numerous platforms and tools available for people to share their stories with a wider audience and in different formats too.

From blogs, podcasts, and social media to virtual reality and augmented reality, there are many ways for people to share their stories and reach a global audience these days.

So, you surely will be making a huge mistake if you are not tapping into this awesome power at your disposal.

Why small businesses need storytelling

As I have already said, you have no reason not to use storytelling in your small business. Studies have shown that stories can be a powerful tool for better community engagement or businesses in terms of marketing, branding, customer engagement, and much more. So, you must allow your small business to benefit from the huge potential of storytelling.

Storytelling is the best instrument to help you refine your voice and build your authority in the global marketplace. Never look down on the power of stories because there is enough scientific evidence that will show you why stories work and how they work.

You can learn more by checking out such valuable publications as "The Science and Power of Storytelling" by the US National Library of Medicine, or "Why Your Brain Loves Good Storytelling" by Paul J. Zak, Harvard Business Review.

Now you need to understand that the human brain is a complex network of billions of communicating neurons, which are connected by chemicals known as neurotransmitters. These neurons work together to transfer information and process it in real-time. The activity of a single neuron, or a small group of neurons, represents a particular feature or aspect of an experience at a given moment.

However, the same neuron or group of neurons, according to researchers and neuron scientists can represent different features at different times because of the many-to-one connectivity. That means multiple neurons can influence a single neuron. What that implies is that a neuron's receptive field, or the information it processes, can change based on the input it receives.

This is important information to know about our behavior so you can better leverage storytelling in what you do. Now, here are 5 good reasons why small business owners need to know about the power of storytelling:

1. **Connection with customers**: Storytelling helps small businesses build an emotional connection with their customers, which can lead to increased brand loyalty and repeat business.
2. **Unique differentiation**: Stories can help small businesses stand out from the competition and showcase their unique personality and values.
3. **Memorable marketing**: Stories are more memorable than traditional advertising and

can leave a lasting impression on customers.
4. **Customer engagement**: Storytelling can engage customers and increase their interest in a small business, leading to greater customer engagement and higher conversion rates.
5. **Building trust**: By sharing stories about their values, beliefs, and experiences, small businesses can build trust and credibility with customers, making them more likely to do business with them.

Yes, small businesses need to know about science-based storytelling so they can better tap into the potential thereof. The complex network of neurons in the brain provides valuable insights into the importance of adaptability and communication in business. It will help you to remember that well.

Stories VS narratives

Yes, there is a difference between a story and a narrative. A story is about the characters and the things that happen to them. In the traditional sense of things, a story should have a beginning, middle, and end, so we can explore the protagonist's dilemmas and choices.

Though they might appear the same, there are differences between a story and a narrative. In one article, the writer puts it brilliantly and it reads:

"Narrative turns story into information, or better, into knowledge for the recipient (the audience or reader). Each story event is a unit of knowledge the audience requires."[15]

You can look at a narrative as a way of observing the world and its influence on us. By that, I mean that a narrative is much bigger than a story. A narrative is constructed from knowledge, beliefs, values, and emotions. Narratives are powerful because they can help us make sense of things that we do not understand or know much about.

Such taglines or symbolic icons like "Just Do It" by Nik or "Think Different" by Apple certainly do not have clear beginnings, middles, or endings like the traditional story, but they offer a glimpse into a world shrouded in powerful messages.

---

[15] *"The easy way to remember the difference between story and narrative is to reshuffle the order of events. A new event order means you have a new narrative of the same story." - Story vs. Narrative - Beemgee.com.*

Come to think of it, millions of people are rallying around those messages and that is a narrative in action.

Stories on the other hand are the building blocks of a narrative. They are what connect the dots, and help the audience understand the bigger picture that is symbolized by such iconic phrases as *"Just Do It"* or *"Think Different"*. A good narrative will use a range of stories to illustrate their point in an easy-to-follow manner. That is what makes storytelling powerful and easily relatable to the audience.

The catch is that, if you do the same with your content creation and small business communication, you are almost guaranteed to have the same effects. Now, here are 7 tips to remember when writing a good story:

1. **Start with a strong hook**: Begin your narrative with a compelling opening that will draw your audience in and make them want to continue reading.
2. **Develop interesting and well-rounded characters**: Make sure your characters are fully fleshed out and believable, with their motivations, desires, and flaws.
3. **Include dialogue**: Including dialogue can help to bring your characters to life and make your story more engaging.
4. **Plan your narrative carefully**: Before you start writing, take some time to brainstorm and outline the events of your story, as well

as the characters and setting. This will help you to stay organized and ensure that your narrative flows smoothly.

5. **Use descriptive language to bring your story to life**: Use good adjectives and adverbs to describe the characters, setting, and events of your story, and use figurative language such as metaphors and similes to add depth and interest.

6. **Consider using good imagery**: Use imagery to engage the reader's senses and help them visualize the story. Consider using descriptive language to help the reader see, hear, smell, taste, and feel what is happening in the story.

7. **Make use of great transitions:** Use better transitions to connect the events of your story and help the narrative flow smoothly. Transitions can be as simple as "then" or "but," or they can be more descriptive, such as "meanwhile" or "as a result."

Overall, always make sure you provide a sense of meaning, direction, and purpose for your story. That is what gives us a broader vision of what is possible if only we are willing to head in that direction. So, yes, there is a difference between a story and a narrative.

As a content creator, either as a podcaster or of other digital content, you can take storytelling even further by controlling the narration and using it in your favor. To be effective in this, make sure your stories are:

- Relatable,
- Impactful,
- And with a good structure.

You don't know what is structure in storytelling? No problem. We will talk about that in the next chapter. So, get ready for it.

Want to learn more about the basics of storytelling? Here are some 5 ways to get started:

1. Start by thinking about your audience and the message you want to convey. What do you want them to take away from your story?
2. Create a clear and concise plot. This should include a beginning, middle, and end, as well as well-defined characters and conflicts.
3. Use expressive language to set the scene and create a visual image in the reader's mind.
4. Use dialogue to reveal character personalities and advance the plot.

Another equally simple but highly important tip is to always revise and edit your work. You need to do that for a more refined story and to make it as strong as possible.

Sometimes, it is not good enough until you have nothing more to take away from your story. Then, you have fully refined your work like a piece of diamond.

Storytelling Guide – The Science Of Storytelling

Here are 5 beginner guides on how to get started with your storytelling:

1. **Identify Your Story**: Determine what story you want to tell and why you want to tell it. This will help you focus your efforts and ensure that your story is relevant and engaging.
2. **Know your audience**: Whether as a small business or content creator, make sure you understand who your story is for, and tailor it to their values, interests, and emotions. This will help you build a better emotional connection with your audience and keep them engaged.
3. **Develop your structure**: Choose a structure that works best for your stories, such as the hero's journey or a linear narrative, to guide the audience through the story and keep them engaged.
4. **Create your characters**: Develop your characters and make them an integral part of the story. Characters help bring the story to life and make it more memorable for your audience.
5. **Practice and refine your work**: Practice telling your story and getting feedback from

other people. Never forget to refine and revise your story until it's more engaging, memorable, and resonates better with your audience. The truth is that, with continued practice, you will eventually become a more skilled and confident storyteller.

Your takeaway from chapter two

Have you ever noticed that the best stories are the ones that stick with you for a longer time? That's because they hit all the right notes. As a content creator or small business owner, make sure you pay attention to these tips.

First, know your audience. It's crucial to understand who you are trying to reach with your story. By tailoring your story to their interests, values, and emotions, you will be able to connect with them on a deeper level.

Next, tap into the emotions. Stories are a great way to build an emotional connection with your audience, and when they feel something, they are more likely to remember your story and even take action.

A clear structure is also important. Think of it as a roadmap that keeps your audience engaged and connected to the story. Don't just tell your story, show it! Use vivid descriptions and sensory details to bring your story to life and engage the audience's imagination.

Another important thing to remember is conflict. Conflict is what drives a story forward, so make sure to add it to your story. Find a conflict that resonates with your audience and keep them hooked from beginning to end.

Finally, end your story with a message. A powerful story should leave a lasting impact on the audience. So, develop the habit of wrapping things up with a meaningful message or lesson for your audience. See you in the next chapter.

CHAPTER 3: ORGANIZING YOUR STORY

Organizing a story is like building a house. Without a solid foundation and a clear plan, the structure will collapse. A guide to organizing your story is like the blueprint for the house, providing the necessary structure and direction for a successful outcome.

Just as a blueprint outlines the rooms and flow of the house, an outline for a story shapes the plot and character arcs. A timeline ensures that each piece of the story falls into place like the bricks of a wall. Distractions and disorganization can be likened to a cluttered construction site, hindering progress, and leading to a messy result and you don't want that.

With the help of a good story organization, writers and content creators can create a cohesive and compelling story that stands strong, like a well-built house. The foundation will be sturdy, the plan will be clear, and the result will be something to be proud of. That is what you want in the end.

Welcome back to Storytelling Basics: How To Get Started In Telling Impactful Stories. This chapter of the book will help you understand why you should organize your story, how to organize your story using different techniques such as the story wheel, how to use storyboarding to organize your story, and most importantly how to go about planning your story before writing.

How do you craft a great story? Well, it all starts with good organization and structure. A well-organized and structured story can be the difference between a captivating narrative and a confusing mess. By using different methods such as outlining, character development charts, and narrative arcs, you can create a better-organized story that will be a pleasure for readers to experience.

Organizing a story is a critical step in the writing process because it helps to structure the narrative and ensure that it flows logically and effectively.

For beginner storytellers who want to better organize their stories, it's important to keep the following guides in mind:

1. **Know your story's beginning, middle, and end**: The beginning sets the scene and introduces the characters, the middle develops the plot and conflicts, and the end provides resolution and closure.
2. **Establish a clear plot structure**: This can be done using a basic 3-act structure or a more complex structure, such as the hero's journey. The structure should guide the story and help you determine where key events should occur.
3. **Develop well-rounded characters**: Make sure your characters have clear motivations, conflicts, and arcs that drive the story forward.
4. **Write clear and concise dialogue**: Dialogue should advance the plot and reveal the characters' personalities, motivations, and emotions. These are what help to connect with the audience.
5. **Make use of the "the show, don't tell" technique**: It is recommended that you use vivid descriptions, actions, and sensory details to show the story's events, rather than simply telling the audience what is happening.

By keeping these tips in mind, you can create a well-structured and engaging story that will hold the reader's interest from beginning to end. Apart from making the story more engaging, having a better organization for your story also makes your job easier. Sure, there are more to why you should consider organizing your story. Let's check that out.

Why should you organize your story?

The task of writing a book can be intimidating, I know, and even some successful authors can struggle with writer's block or too many ideas for their next project. However, by learning how to organize their ideas, fiction, and nonfiction writers alike can save time, effort, and stress in the long run. By having a clear starting point, they can focus on their writing, resulting in a smoother book-writing process.

In all my books, my typical approach begins with the selection of the topic I wish to explore. Once I have settled on the subject matter, my next step is to craft an outline. This initial framework sets the stage for the entire writing journey, providing a structured path to follow.

Of course, this doesn't mean it's a rigid process; it often involves a series of reviews, adjustments, and adaptations as I progress. However, I find immense satisfaction in this method because it affords me a well-defined plan of action. This clarity allows me to channel my creative energies effectively, from the inception of the project right through to its completion. And I encourage you to do the same.

Organizing your story before writing can help you create a more effective and engaging narrative flow that will hold the reader's interest and convey your message more effectively. Now, here are more reasons you should consider organizing a story before writing:

1. Organizing your story helps to create a clear and structured narrative that is easy for the reader to follow.
2. It ensures that the plot, characters, and themes are coherent and consistent throughout the story.
3. Organizing your story allows the writer to identify and eliminate unnecessary or redundant elements, resulting in a tighter and more impactful story.
4. It provides a roadmap for the writer, reducing the likelihood of getting stuck or losing the thread of the story.
5. Organizing your story makes it easier to see the big picture and identify areas that need further development or improvement.

With that now understood, let's consider some of the best ways to organize your story because there are different ways to achieve the same result. I want to repeat that: all of us are not the same so, the method that works for one might not work for another and certainly not in the same way. So, you need to see which of them will work better for you.

Organizing your story with the story wheel

Do you often find yourself struggling to come up with story ideas? If so, you are not alone. You can approach the organization of your story ideas by using a tool I find very effective, the "Story Wheel".

A story wheel is a tool that helps writers organize their story ideas. It is a visual map that breaks down the elements of a story into different categories. These categories are broad enough to ensure the writer has many options with which to work and you can use the same approach either for a book project, a film, or any other creative work.

Here is how to organize your story, using the story wheel:

1. **Plot Points**: Use the Story Wheel to organize and track the key plot points in your story, such as inciting incidents, rising action, climax, and resolution. This will help you ensure that your story has a clear narrative arc and that all the elements perfectly fit together.
2. **Character Development**: Using the Story Wheel can help you map out your characters' journeys, including their

motivations, conflicts, and growth. This will help you make sure that your characters are well-rounded and effectively drive the story forward.

3. **Themes**: You can also use the Story Wheel to visualize and connect themes in your story. This will help you ensure that your themes are consistent and that they support the story's overall message.

4. **Setting**: Use the Story Wheel to map out the setting and how it changes over time. This will help you create a vivid and immersive world for your story and ensure that the setting supports the story's overall goals.

5. **Symbolism**: Use the Story Wheel to identify and connect symbols in your story. This will help you create a rich and layered narrative, where each symbol adds depth and meaning to the story.

A story wheel is useful for understanding how stories are composed, helped by imagination, and oral language skills. It's also a helpful resource for organizing your own story, especially when the plotline is not clear enough to you in the beginning.

Use storyboarding to organize your story

Storyboarding is a visual tool that is used to organize and plan a story before writing. It involves creating a series of illustrations or sketches that represent key scenes in the story. If done correctly, storyboarding can help to map out the narrative and visualize the story's structure more clearly.

Here's how you can use storyboarding to organize your story:

1. **Sketch out the key scenes**: Use simple illustrations or rough sketches to map out the key scenes in your story. Considering including the beginning, middle, and end.
2. **Add notes**: Write notes or brief descriptions of what happens in each scene to help you remember the details. The devil, they say, is in the details.
3. **Create a visual timeline**: Arrange the scenes in the order in which they occur, and this will help you to create a visual timeline of the story.
4. **Identify gaps or areas for improvement**: Review the storyboard and identify any gaps or areas that need further development or improvement to make the story stand out.

Example: If you were writing a story about a detective solving a murder case, your storyboard might look something like this:

- Scene 1: Detective introduced and assigned to a murder case,

- Scene 2: Detective interviews witnesses and collects evidence,
- Scene 3: The detective discovers a clue that leads to a suspect,
- Scene 4: The detective interrogates the suspect and gathers more evidence,
- Scene 5: The detective solves the case and makes an arrest.

This visual representation of your story can help you see the overall flow and structure of your narrative, making it easier to identify any issues and make improvements before writing the first draft. That is the power of organizing your story through storyboarding.

Organize your story with index cards

Organizing a story with index cards is a simple and effective way to plan your narrative before writing. Index cards allow you to easily rearrange and manipulate the elements of your story, helping you to identify and eliminate unnecessary elements, and ensuring that your story flows logically.

Here's how you can use index cards to organize your story as a beginner:

1. **Write one scene per card**: Write a summary of each scene on an individual index card, focusing on the key events, characters, and dialogue.

2. **Arrange the cards**: Lay out the index cards in the order in which the scenes occur. Doing it this way will allow you to visualize the structure and flow of your story.
3. **Add notes**: Because they are separate, you can easily use the back of the cards to jot down notes, ideas, or additional details that you may need later.
4. **Reorder the cards**: Based on your needs, you can easily rearrange the cards to make changes to the story structure. With the story now up visually, you can try out different variations until you have a coherent and engaging narrative.

Example: If you were writing a story about a young chef trying to save his family's restaurant business, your index cards might look something like this:

- Card 1: Chef is introduced, and a restaurant is facing financial trouble,
- Card 2: Chef creates a new menu and raises money to fix the kitchen,
- Card 3: Chef discovers a hidden talent for cooking and wins a local competition,
- Card 4: The Chef gets an invitation to cook at a prestigious restaurant and struggles with decisions,
- Card 5: Chef decides to stay and save the family restaurant and wins the support of customers.

Organizing your story with index cards allows you to easily experiment with different structures, identify areas for improvement, and ensure that your story is well-structured and engaging before you start writing your first draft.

Organize your story with mind-mapping

is a creative and visual tool used to organize and plan a story. It involves creating a diagram that shows the relationships between different ideas, concepts, and characters in a story. It's one of the most effective ways for writers to organize their stories and create a more coherent and logical narration.

Here's how you can use mind mapping to organize your story:

1. **Start with a central idea**: Write the main concept or theme of your story in the center of a blank page and draw a circle around it.
2. **Add branches**: Draw branches or lines from the central idea and write key elements of your story such as characters, settings, or events.
3. **Connect ideas**: Draw connections between the different elements of your story, showing how they relate to each other and the central idea.

4. **Add details**: You can expand each branch with additional details, such as character traits, dialogue, or sensory details.
5. **Refine and edit**: Review your mind map, and make changes or revisions as needed to improve the flow and coherence of your story.

Example: If you were writing a story about a young girl who discovers a magical world, your mind map might look something like this:

- Identify the central idea of a young girl who discovers a magical world,
- Branch 1: Main character, personality traits,
- Branch 2: Magical world, location, and creatures,
- Branch 3: Journey through the magical world, obstacles, and allies,
- Branch 4: Conflict and battle against evil,
- Branch 5: Resolution and return to the normal world.

Mind mapping allows you to visually organize the elements of your story and explore the relationships between them. This makes it easier to identify and eliminate unnecessary elements and improves the overall structure of your narrative.

Now, let's talk about something equally fundamental, not only within storytelling but in everything you do. That is planning as said by Confucius, the Chinese philosopher, "A man who does not plan long ahead will find trouble at his door." So, make sure you plan your story. Let's learn more about that.

Planning your story

To successfully tell a story, you need to plan it well in advance. This will allow you to create an outline for your story that will help you write more efficiently and with more clarity.

This means you will have a better idea of where your story is going and how it should be structured. For more about story structure, remember what we discussed earlier about the structuring of a story. Consider the following tips if you want to successfully plan your story:

➤ What are you trying to communicate?

There's nothing more compelling than a good story. As you start brainstorming, it can help to ask yourself what kind of story you are trying to tell. This could be a one-line pitch or a question you are trying to answer for your audience.

For example, Romeo and Juliet could be pitched as 'the tragic story of star-crossed lovers whose love was forbidden and whose relationship was doomed to fail'. Can you do the same with the story you want to tell? You get the point.

> ## Consider writing the cover blurb of your story

Before you start to write a story, have an idea of what you want your characters to experience and why along with some key plot points. This will help the reader better understand your story and the events that happen.

You should think of telling a friend about your story before you start writing it. This process can help you identify the most important parts of your story and keep them consistent with each other. It also helps to make sure that there's a coherent plotline to follow throughout the narration.

> ## Know the characters you are presenting in the story

This is fundamental for successful storytelling. It will serve you well to make a list of the major and minor characters when planning out your story. To create a list of major and minor characters, outline with some details of each one as follows:

- Name,
- Age,
- Physical appearance,
- Beliefs, and more.

Will your protagonist regret that they never embraced their talent enough and settled for what worked? Would they have thrown away every opportunity because they were afraid to fail? Knowing these ahead of time will help you to better plan your story.

Storytelling guide - Organizing your story

I understand that writing a compelling story can be a daunting task sometimes. But with the right organizational skills, it's possible to create an engaging narrative that can capture the attention of your readers.

As in the case of most successful writers out there, using simple tips and tricks, you can easily organize your story in a way that will make it easier to read and understand. Now, here are 10 guides on how to organize your story for effective impact:

1. **Start with a clear concept**: This will provide a focus and direction for the story.

2. **Create an outline**: A basic outline will help you keep track of the plot and ensure a logical flow.
3. **Develop the characters and their motivations**: Well-rounded characters will drive the story and create conflict.
4. **Build tension and conflict**: This is what drives the story forward and keeps the reader engaged.
5. **Use foreshadowing and flashbacks wisely**: These devices can add depth and meaning to the story.
6. **Ensure that there is a clear beginning, middle, and end**: A good story needs a well-defined narrative structure to be effective.
7. **Maintain consistency in tone, style, and pacing**: Do not underestimate this because it will help maintain the reader's engagement and create a cohesive story.
8. **Consider using symbols**: As mentioned earlier, using some element of symbolism can add additional layers of meaning to the story.
9. **Revise and edit multiple times**: Rewriting and editing are essential for refining and improving the story.
10. **Get feedback from beta readers or a critique group**: This is important if you want to grow. Getting fresh perspectives from beta readers (test readers of your unreleased work) can help identify weaknesses and suggest possible improvements.

Your takeaway from chapter three

With the right organization, writing your stories can be made much easier. It's therefore recommended that you break down your story into manageable sections and effectively organize them. That will help create a clear and more powerful narrative.

Understanding the importance of story organization and flow is essential to writing a great story, so take the time to plan out your plot points, characters, dialogue, and settings to craft an impactful story.

In this chapter, you also had the chance to learn about why you should organize your story and the different techniques of story organization. If you have any need, you can always come back to reread this chapter because you are going to need it to successfully craft your stories.

The next chapter is about "Story Structure" which is an equally essential part of successful storytelling. So, get ready for it.

CHAPTER 4: THE STORY STRUCTURE

Writing a story without a structure is like building a house without a foundation. No matter how impressive the design, it's bound to crumble without a strong base to hold it up.

From the framework of the plot to the structure of the characters, great storytelling needs a sturdy foundation for the narrative to stand.

Look at it like a house that needs solid walls, a roof, and a solid foundation to stand the test of time. A good story requires a solid structure to capture and hold the reader's attention. There cannot be any denial of that.

Welcome back to Storytelling Basics: How To Get Started In Telling Impactful Stories. I want to believe you have attempted the exercise in the last chapter. Now, let's move into the conversation of this chapter, the story structure.

By the end of this chapter, you should be able to understand what structure in storytelling is, how to structure your story, and what makes a good three-act structure. You need this understanding to better leverage structure in your stories.

What is the structure of storytelling?

The structure in storytelling refers to the organization and arrangement of the elements in a narrative, which helps to convey a coherent and engaging story to the audience.

There are various approaches to structuring a story, but one of the most common and widely recognized structures is the three-act structure, often used in screenplays, novels, and other forms of storytelling. We will talk more about the three-act structure later in this chapter of the book.

The story structure, sometimes referred to as narrative structure, can also be the order in which events are organized:

- Beginning,
- Middle,
- And ending in a story.

A story's structure directly affects the way the plot unfolds. It determines whether your story will be a tragedy or a comedy.

To put it differently, the structure of a story is the foundation for everything that follows. The first sentence, paragraph, chapter, and so on are all built up to form the final narrative. There are some characteristics a good story structure must have. Here are 6 of them for your consideration:

1. **Clear and concise plot**: A good story should have a clear and concise plot that is easy to follow and understand. This means that there should be a clear beginning, middle, and end, with a strong conflict or problem to be resolved.
2. **Interesting and well-developed characters**: A Good story should have well-developed characters that are interesting and believable. These characters should have their own motivations, desires, and flaws, and should change and grow throughout the story.
3. **Engaging dialogue**: A good story should have dialogue that is interesting, and realistic, and helps to advance the plot and develop the characters.
4. **A consistent and believable setting**: The setting of a story should be consistent and believable and should help to enhance the atmosphere and mood of the story.
5. **A satisfying resolution**: For a story to be considered good, it needs to have a

satisfying resolution that resolves the main conflict or problem in a believable and meaningful way.

6. **Thematic depth**: All good stories should have deeper themes or messages that give them meaning and resonance beyond just the surface-level plot.

Structure plays a crucial role in storytelling as it provides a framework for the narrative. It determines the pacing, reveals the plot, and helps to build tension and suspense. A well-structured story keeps the audience engaged and helps to guide their emotional journey.

The structure can also reveal character development, foreshadow events, and create surprises for the audience. In short, the structure acts as a backbone to the story, giving it shape and direction, and it's an essential component of all storytelling.

In an interesting article, the writer stated, and I quote:

> *"We believe a powerful story should have readers wanting to know what happens next while taking the main character on an*

emotional and spiritual journey of change."[16]

I came across the article through short research online. I needed to refresh my head about the topic, and it turned out to be a good read. You too can consider reading the full story, "The Power Of Structure" at Writerstudio.com.

To write a successful story, make sure you have a strong beginning. A strong beginning means that it should be interesting enough to keep people hooked and reading through to the end.

Of course, your middle should be good by tapping into such techniques as suspense and some element of conflict, so as not to remain flat and boring to the audience.

As correctly put by the American nonfiction writer, journalist, and former fiction editor at The New Yorker, Bill Buford: "Of the many definitions of story, the simplest may be this. It is a piece of

---

[16] *"Structure and character are two sides to one coin. One exists to reveal the other. This is the fundamental basis to classic story structure." - The Power Of Structure - Writerstudio.com.*

writing that makes the reader want to find out what happens next." And Good writers, he added, "have the ability to make you keep on reading them whether you want to or not — the milk boils over — the subway stop is missed..." If you have ever enjoyed a good story, you should understand what Bill is talking about here.

When it comes to properly structuring your storytelling, Robert B. Cialdini, professor of psychology at Arizona State University said it perfectly as follows:

> "Mystery grabs readers by the collar and pulls them into the material. When structured properly, mysteries are so compelling that the reader cannot remain and aloof and neutral outside observer of the story's form and structure."

So, the structure is also all about the way you set up the story elements, like delicate traps to trigger the emotions of your audience so they can remain at the edge of their seats, waiting for what will happen next.

If you have read the book "Things Fall Apart", referenced earlier at the beginning of this book, you will understand how masterfully Chinua Achebe executed this. You could literally hold your breath in chapter 7 of the book, waiting to see what will happen to the fate of Ikemefuna.

Ikemefuna, who has developed a close bond with Okonkwo like a son, meets a tragic end at Okonkwo's hands. Despite receiving precise instructions not to directly engage in Ikemefuna's execution, Okonkwo ultimately strikes him down with a machete when Ikemefuna rushes toward him. That is certainly not a part to be forgotten hastily in the book.

Learning how to structure your story properly will serve you well in taking your audience from the beginning to the end of your story. Never forget that a strong ending in a story satisfies readers by answering any questions they may have had throughout the work. Do that well and you will be your audience's favorite.

Talking of a good story, there are about 7 basic elements to every successful storytelling, and they are as follows:

1. A compelling protagonist,
2. A clear sense of what the protagonist wants and how this relates to the conflict,
3. A plot that is driven by a series of escalating events,
4. A setting that is vivid, specific, and appropriate to the plot,
5. Dialogue that reveals character and moves the story forward,
6. Descriptions of what the characters think and feel about each other and themselves,
7. And a satisfying ending.

Make sure you take those into consideration when creating your stories. Now, let's consider how to go about structuring your storytelling. This should be a vital part of this chapter of the book.

How to structure your story

The question of how to correctly structure your story is a fundamental one if you want to be a successful storyteller and stand out from the noise out there. As already stated, the structure of a story is one of the most important aspects of storytelling. It is what makes us want to read or stop reading a book altogether.

To understand the narrative structure, it is important to know that there are different types to it as follows:

Linear structure

Linear narratives are those events that follow a storyline in chronological order and have a clear beginning, middle, and end. In the last chapter of this book, we will refer to the chronological order of storytelling when we shall be talking about the NBA storytelling technique. Just keep that in mind.

The chronological order of storytelling usually follows a straightforward timeline, and the events unfold in the order in which they occur. This type of story structure is straightforward to follow, and it helps to build suspense and anticipation as the story progresses.

It can also make character arcs and plot twists more impactful, as the audience experiences events in real time with the characters. Some examples of linear structured stories are:

- Pride & Prejudice by Jane Austen,
- The History of Tom Jones by Henry Fielding,
- Anna Karenina by Leo Tolstoy and more.

Non-linear structure

The non-linear stories, on the other hand, tend not to follow a strict timeline and can be more complicated than most linear ones. In a non-linear structure, the story may jump back and forth in time, or present events in a fragmented manner. This type of structure adds complexity to the story and can be used to create suspense, reveal character development, or explore multiple perspectives.

However, the non-linear structure can be challenging for audiences as it requires more effort to piece together the events, but it can also be more engaging and thought-provoking. It can create a sense of unpredictability, making the audience more invested in the story.

Here are some examples of non-linear structured stories:

- Wuthering Heights by Emily Brontë,
- Slaughterhouse-Five by Kurt Vonnegut,
- Story of Your Life by Novella by Ted Chiang.

Other types of narrative structures to consider include:

- **Viewpoint narrative**: The viewpoint narrative is typically a type of literary narration attributed to the protagonist's perspective in the story. The reader can find out about the key events in the story through the character's thoughts, emotions, and actions. The protagonist is usually a major player in the story, but not always.
- **Quest narrative**: In a quest narrative, the hero strives hard and faces huge odds to achieve their goal. The quest they undertake becomes their all-consuming passion, and they must fight against insurmountable odds to obtain it.
- **Circular narrative**: In a circular narrative, the story starts and ends at the same point, but the character undergoes some changes due to the events of the story. Circular storytelling is a great method that can be used to structure the plot and narrative of a story.

To create good stories, your narrative structure should tell a story. It should help you organize the plot points and reveal them gradually to the readers.

Most stories often have a single question as the focus of the narrative. Think of the following questions and you will quickly remember the entire story that was built around each of them:

- Will Harry Potter defeat Voldemort?
- Could Romeo and Juliet end up together?
- Could Frodo destroy the Ring?

The narrative structure of a story is created by the series of events that follow the original important question. This is why it is essential to structure your story the right way and that takes us to three the three-act structure. Let's see to that and how you can apply it in your storytelling.

The three-act structure

The three-act structure is a storytelling framework used in the planning and execution of a narrative, be it a novel, movie, play, or other forms of storytelling. It's usually comprised of three parts or acts as follows:

1. **Act I - Introduction and setup:** The first act introduces the main characters, the setting, and the main conflict of the story. This act sets the stage for the hero's

journey and ends with an inciting incident that propels the hero into action.

2. **Act II - Confrontation and conflict:** In this act, the heroes are faced with challenges and obstacles as they work towards resolving the main conflict of the story. This act builds tension and raises the stakes, and the hero's journey reaches its climax.

3. **Act III - Resolution and conclusion:** In the final act, the hero faces the final challenge and resolves the main conflict. This act ties up loose ends and provides closure to the story, often with a moral, lesson learned, or the key message for the audience to take home.

The science behind the three-act structure

The three-act structure is a storytelling framework that has its roots in classical dramatic theory and has been widely adopted in various forms of narrative media. The structure, as already stated, divides a narrative into three main parts: the setup, confrontation, and resolution.

The science behind the three-act structure lies in its alignment with the natural rhythms of human cognition and emotional engagement. Psychologically, humans tend to seek patterns and structure in the information they receive. The three-act structure provides a coherent and predictable narrative framework that mirrors the way individuals perceive and process information.

The setup, confrontation, and resolution align with the audience's expectations for a beginning, middle, and end, creating a sense of order and satisfaction. The rising action in the second act generates tension, triggering emotional responses and maintaining the audience's interest.

This structure has proven effective in holding attention, enhancing comprehension, and fostering emotional engagement. This is what makes it a valuable tool in the art and science of storytelling.

In addition, the three-act structure is rooted in the concept of narrative tension and release, which corresponds to the ebb and flow of emotional engagement. The setup introduces the characters and their world, creating a baseline level of interest.

The confrontation, with its rising action and escalating conflicts, heightens tension and draws the audience deeper into the narrative. This tension is a crucial element, as it keeps the audience emotionally invested and eager to see how the story unfolds.

The resolution then provides the release, offering a satisfying conclusion and fulfilling the emotional expectations set up in the preceding acts. This rhythmic alternation between tension and release aligns with psychological theories of storytelling, suggesting that effective narratives mimic the natural cadence of human emotional experiences, making them more resonant and memorable.

In essence, the three-act structure leverages the interplay of tension and release to create a captivating and emotionally satisfying storytelling experience. Now, here are three movie examples that perfectly follow the three-act structure:

1. **The Terminator" (1984):** This sci-fi classic follows the three-act structure, with Act 1 establishing the protagonist Sarah Connor, and the threat of the Terminator. Act 2 shows Sarah's attempts to evade the Terminator and understand the situation, and Act 3 resolves the conflict as Sarah and Kyle Reese team up to defeat the Terminator.
2. **Forrest Gump" (1994):** This beloved comedy-drama follows the three-act structure, with Act 1 introducing Forrest Gump and establishing his life story. Act 2 shows Forrest's journey through some of the defining events of the 20th century, and Act 3 resolves the conflict as Forrest finds peace and happiness in his life.
3. **Indiana Jones and the Raiders of the Lost Ark" (1981):** This adventure classic follows the three-act structure, with Act 1

introducing Indiana Jones and establishing the quest for the Ark of the Covenant. Act 2 shows Indiana's journey to find the Ark, and Act 3 resolves the conflict with a showdown as Indiana retrieves the Ark and defeats the villains.

These movies use the three-act structure to create a clear and engaging narrative, building tension and suspense as the story progresses, and ultimately satisfyingly resolving the conflict.

The three-act structure is a flexible framework that can be adapted to fit the specific needs of a particular story. It provides a roadmap for the story's progression and helps to ensure that the narrative is well-paced, engaging, and satisfying for the audience.

What makes a good three-act structure?

You want to use a three-act structure in your story. Right? Good, but first you need to understand the characteristics and traits that make it effective, and they are as follows:

1. **Clear set-up**: The first act must effectively establish the main characters, the setting, and the main conflict, thereby creating a clear picture for the audience of what to expect from the story.

2. **Rising tension**: The second act should build tension and increase the stakes, keeping the audience engaged and invested in the hero's journey.
3. **Satisfying resolution**: The final act must provide a satisfying resolution to the main conflict, tying up loose ends and leaving the audience with a sense of closure.
4. **Well-paced progression**: A good three-act structure should have a well-paced progression, with each act building on the previous one and driving the story forward.
5. **Engaging character arc**: The hero's journey and personal transformation should be a key part of the three-act structure, with the hero's character arc serving as a central theme throughout the story.

It's also a good idea to consider effective plot points and a clear theme. By incorporating these elements into your story, you can create a good three-act structure that is a well-rounded, engaging, and satisfying story for the audience. The other types of structure to consider as often used both in books and movies are:

- Parallel structure,
- Circular plot structure,
- And an interactive plot structure.

Now, let's understand them each and some examples of where they have been used in books and movies.

Parallel structure

The parallel structure in storytelling refers to the repetition of similar grammatical forms, words, or phrases in a sequence of sentences or clauses. It creates a sense of balance and coherence and helps to emphasize the relationships between ideas.

The parallel structure can be used in dialogue, description, and other elements of a story to create a rhythmic and cohesive narrative.

This can happen through the repetition of the same verb, tense, or sentence structure in a series of sentences to create a sense of parallelism, thereby making the writing feel more organized and intentional. Are you looking for examples in popular movies? Here are three for your consideration:

- **The Lion King (1994):** In the opening scene, Rafiki says, "The sun will rise on a new day, and the youthful will be king." This repetition of "will rise" and "will be" creates a sense of parallelism, emphasizing the coming of a new era.
- **The Dark Knight (2008):** In one of the most famous scenes, the Joker says, "Why

so serious?" This phrase is repeated throughout the film and becomes a signature catchphrase, creating a sense of parallel structure that ties the story together.

- **The Matrix (1999):** The character Morpheus repeatedly says, "Unfortunately, no one can be told what the Matrix is. You have to see it for yourself." This repetition of the phrase "you have to see it for yourself" creates a sense of parallel structure, emphasizing the idea that the Matrix cannot be fully understood without personal experience.

Circular plot structure

Circular plot structure in storytelling is a narrative technique where the ending of the story is closely connected to the beginning, thereby creating a sense of circularity or completion.

This type of plot structure creates a cyclical pattern, where the story ends in a similar way to how it started. This often brings the narrative to a full circle.

This type of structure can add a sense of resolution, symmetry, and closure to a story, and can also create a more memorable narrative that lingers with the reader or viewer, depending on the format of the story.

For example, a circular plot structure may involve a protagonist who begins and ends the story in the same place, or with the same realization. The circular structure emphasizes the idea that the journey is more important than the destination and that the story's events are interconnected.

Here are 5 characteristics of circular plot structure in storytelling:

1. **Beginning and end are connected**: The story starts and ends similarly or identically.
2. **Cyclical pattern**: The story creates a sense of cyclicality, with events recurring in a repetitive pattern.
3. **Full circle resolution**: The story resolves in a way that brings the narrative full circle, thereby creating a sense of closure.
4. **The journey is emphasized**: The focus is on the protagonist's journey and the events that occur along the way, rather than the destination.
5. **Interconnected events**: The events of the story are interconnected, forming a cohesive narrative.

Interactive plot structure

Interactive plot structure in storytelling is a narrative technique where the reader, viewer, or player is directly involved in the outcome of the story. This type of structure is often used in video games, interactive novels, and other forms of interactive media, where the user can make choices that affect the direction of the story.

The interactive plot structure creates a sense of agency and ownership, allowing the user to shape the story in unique and personal ways. This can be very useful, especially if you want to encourage more active participation from your audience as against being passive. We will talk more about the audience in later parts of this five-part book series. So, look out for that.

In an interactive plot structure, the user's choices determine the course of the story, leading to a wide range of possible outcomes and multiple possible endings. This type of plot structure can increase engagement and immersion, as the user is actively involved in the story, rather than simply observing it.

Do you want to correctly use an interactive plot structure in your story? Here are some good book examples to consider and hopefully learn from:

- **Choose your adventure series:** This popular series of books allows the reader to make choices that determine the outcome of the story. Each choice leads to a different page, allowing the reader to explore different paths and endings in their interaction.

- **The Witcher video game series:** The Witcher video games allow the player to make choices that affect the direction of the story and the relationships between the characters. The player's decisions have consequences that shape the outcome of the story, leading to multiple possible endings.
- **The Magician's Nephew" by C.S. Lewis:** This book is part of The Chronicles of Narnia series and features an interactive plot structure that allows the reader to shape the story by making choices for the characters. The reader can choose to follow the path of good or evil, leading to different endings and outcomes.

Depending on the type of story you are telling, any of the above examples can work for you. So, feel free to experiment with them and that leads us to the storytelling guide for this chapter.

Storytelling guide – Story structure

Do you want to create a compelling structure? Here are some of the best strategies to adopt, based on what we have discussed in this chapter of the book:

1. **Know your story's genre**: Understanding the conventions and expectations of your story's genre can help you create a structure that is both familiar and effective.

2. **Consider your story's themes**: Think about the central themes and messages of your story, and how you can structure your plot to support and emphasize these ideas.
3. **Plan your plot points**: It will serve you well to map out the key events and turning points of your story. Consider also how you can arrange them logically and compellingly.
4. **Use cause and effect**: You can also consider how events and actions in your story are connected, and how one event leads to another in a causal chain.
5. **Read and analyze successful stories**: Of course, this is fundamental. Reading the stories of other writers within your genre or even from other genres can be a great strategy for your learning process. When you do this, make sure to take note of their structures, and the elements that make them engaging and effective.
6. **Experiment with different structures**: Don't be afraid to try different structures and see what might work best for your story. Remember, there is no one wrong or right structure to use in your stories. You may need to try several storytelling structures before finding the one that can work best for your story.

Your takeaway from Chapter Four

Story structure is the backbone of any successful narrative. It helps to create an engaging story arc that captivates the readers and keeps them interested in the story. It also provides a framework for characters and plot points, allowing the writer to craft a cohesive and convincing story.

By understanding and applying the basic principles of story structure as we have discussed in this chapter, writers can create compelling stories that will resonate with their readers for years to come.

CHAPTER 5: THE HERO'S JOURNEY

Embark on a journey of self-discovery with "THE HERO'S JOURNEY." Do you want to explore the timeless storytelling archetype that has captivated audiences for centuries? You will not regret it.

From ancient myths to modern-day blockbusters, the hero's journey is a blueprint for creating compelling and transformative stories. By understanding the hero's journey, you can craft characters that truly resonate with your audiences and build narratives that leave a lasting impact.

Do not underestimate the hero's journey archetype and why it has captivated audiences since the days of old.

Welcome to Chapter 5 of the book, Storytelling Basics: How To Get Started In Telling Impactful Stories. In this chapter of the book, we will learn about The Hero's Journey.

By the end of this chapter, you should understand what the hero's journey is, how to use the hero's journey in business, and how to write a great hero's journey that will keep your audience at the edge of their seats.

What is the hero's journey?

The hero's journey is a timeless narrative structure that is used to tell the story of a hero's quest for success. The hero embarks on a journey to achieve a goal, facing trials and obstacles along the way, and finally achieving the reward.

The hero's journey can be found in a wide range of stories, from classic myths to modern-day films and books. It's equally a great type of story to tell in business. You will understand why that is the case later in this book, and other parts of the five-part book series when we shall be specific about business.

At its core, the hero's journey is about growth, transformation, and fulfillment. The hero is presented with a call to adventure, which he/she may initially resist but eventually embrace. Through their journey, they face challenges and obstacles that help them develop and mature, preparing them for the final push toward their goal.

The heroes reach the climax of their journey as they approach the inmost cave, where they must overcome their greatest challenge. Finally, the hero achieves the reward, which represents the satisfaction of a job well done.

The hero's journey usually contains 12 distinct steps that the hero must endure in three parts: Departure, Initiation, and Return. Now, here are the 12 steps a hero's journey typically takes. You, surely, might already see these in movies or books, so pay attention to better identify them:

1. **The spark:** The hero gets a thrilling invitation to embark on an adventure.
2. **The resistance:** At first, the hero is hesitant to leave his or her comfort zone and embrace the unknown.
3. **The guide:** Along the way, the hero meets a wise mentor who provides guidance and support.
4. **The leap of faith:** The hero decides to take the plunge and cross the threshold into the unknown.
5. **The trials:** The hero faces obstacles, makes new allies, and battles enemies on the journey.
6. **The dark night:** The hero reaches a crucial turning point and must navigate through a dangerous situation, physical or emotional.

7. **The epic battle:** The hero faces the toughest challenge yet, putting his/her skills and courage to the test.
8. **The triumph:** The hero emerges victorious, receiving a prize or gaining new insights.
9. **The homeward bound:** The hero starts the journey back to their ordinary life, facing new obstacles along the way.
10. **The transformation:** The hero experiences a final, defining moment that symbolizes a change within them.
11. **The gift:** The hero returns home with a valuable lesson learned or a gift to share with others.
12. **The legend:** The hero has completed his/her journey and has gained the wisdom and power to navigate both the ordinary and extraordinary worlds.

This is my recommendation for you: look at these 12 steps carefully and see how you can apply them in your stories. If you understand the process, you can successfully set up your characters on a transformative journey filled with trials and tribulations, and ultimately lead them to true enlightenment.

That makes you a professional story writer. And talking of being a professional story writer, let's look more into how to write a great hero's journey and this time for your business.

Using a hero's journey in business

The hero's journey can be an effective tool for businesses to create a compelling and engaging narrative. To use the hero's journey in a business setting, identify the problem or challenge that the business is facing, create a hero (such as the business itself, an employee, or a customer), and establish the call to action.

Throughout the journey, the hero will encounter various trials and obstacles, learning important lessons and becoming stronger in the process. The journey concludes with the hero achieving the reward or outcome, which can be framed as the success of the business or the satisfaction of the customers.

Here are 3 good examples of different companies that have successfully used the hero's journey. Perhaps, there is something you can learn from them:

➢ *Tesla, Inc*

Tesla's mission to accelerate the world's transition to sustainable energy can be seen as a hero's journey. The company's CEO, Elon Musk, is often portrayed as a visionary and a hero, leading the charge to create a better future for humanity.

With its electric vehicles, solar products, and energy storage solutions, Tesla is overcoming trials and obstacles, such as the skepticism of traditional auto and energy industries, to create a cleaner and more sustainable world.

What is the reward? Well, it is the satisfaction of contributing to a greener future and creating a positive impact on the environment.

➢ *Patagonia, Inc.*

Through the hero journey, Patagonia, the outdoor clothing, and gear company has successfully positioned itself as a protagonist in the world of sustainability and environmental activism. With its commitment to using sustainable materials and practices, Patagonia is on a journey to protect the environment and create a better world for future generations.

The company's trials and obstacles include the challenges of operating in a largely unsustainable industry, but Patagonia's commitment to sustainability and its use of activism as a tool to drive change has made it a leader in the field.

What about the satisfaction? Patagonia's satisfaction is creating a positive impact on the environment and inspiring others to do the same. That is a great mission that is worth pursuing. Don't you agree?

➤ *Warby Parker*

Based in New York City, Warby Parker is an American online retailer of medicated glasses, contact lenses, and sunglasses. The company has positioned itself as a hero in the world of affordable fashion and social responsibility. The company's journey to create stylish, affordable eyewear and give back to the community is one of great purpose and impact.

By offering stylish glasses and sunglasses at affordable prices, Warby Parker is overcoming the trials and obstacles of an industry that has traditionally been focused on luxury and exclusivity. Their satisfaction is making a positive impact on people's lives and providing access to quality eye care for all.

What can you do? Well, by using the hero's journey this way, you can create a cohesive and inspiring story that motivates and unites people around your business.

It can make both customers and stakeholders forge a common goal with you. With that out of the way, how do you write the hero journey type of story? Let's see to that because it's vital if you want to succeed.

Key benefits of the Hero's journey story

Remember that the hero's journey begins with the departure when the hero leaves their ordinary world behind and embarks on an adventure. This is often when they are presented with an obstacle or challenge to overcome.

From there, they will experience trials and tribulations as they make their way to the ultimate climax of their journey. I understand that this can be challenging for beginners, but with the right guidance, you can create an inspiring and captivating story that will capture your reader's attention and take them through a thrilling journey of ups and downs.

Another reason you should understand how to construct a good hero's journey story as a business owner is that it's very common in the business ecosystem, especially for marketing purposes. And if you are going to be doing marketing, you should know how it works.

As a small business owner, learning about the hero's journey structure can bring several key benefits to your sales approach such as:

1. **Understanding your audience**: By using the hero's journey as a framework, you can better understand your target audience's needs and desires, and craft content that

speaks directly to them. You can use the structure to highlight the challenges and obstacles your audience faces and show them how your products or services can help.

2. **Emotional appeal**: The hero's journey is an emotional story structure that evokes a range of emotions in the reader. By tapping into this emotional appeal, you can easily create a strong connection with your audience and increase the chances of your business's success.

3. **Differentiation**: The hero's journey is a well-known structure, and by using it in your unique way, you can differentiate yourself from your competition and stand out in a crowded market.

4. **Consistency**: The hero's journey provides a clear and consistent structure that can be used across all your marketing materials, including website copy, email campaigns, and video content. This consistency helps to build a strong brand image and increase brand recognition.

Overall, incorporating the hero's journey structure into your content creation and sales approach can help you create more engaging and effective content. It will help you understand your audience better and stand out in your market.

Storytelling guide – The Hero's Journey

Here are some of the characteristics of the hero's journey:

1. **It's a universal story structure**: The hero's journey is a universal story structure that has been used for centuries to tell stories across cultures and genres.
2. **It follows a 12-step pattern**: The hero's journey is comprised of 12 stages that follow a clear and distinct pattern, from the hero's call to adventure to their return home.
3. **It focuses on the hero's transformation**: The hero's journey is centered around the hero's transformation and growth, from an ordinary person to a hero.
4. **It invokes emotional responses**: Another great quality of the hero's journey is that it's designed to evoke a range of emotions in the reader or viewer, from fear and uncertainty to triumph and fulfillment.
5. **It's adaptable**: While the hero's journey is a well-established structure, it is flexible and can be adapted to fit the specific needs of a particular story or genre. The key is to stay true to the underlying principles of the hero's journey and use them in a way that serves the story.

Your takeaway from Chapter Five

Think of the hero's journey as a roadmap for storytelling. Just as a roadmap guides a traveler from point A to point B, the hero's journey provides a structure for telling a story that takes the hero from their everyday life to a transformative experience.

As we learned in this chapter of the book, the hero's journey includes trials and obstacles that help the hero grow and mature. And just as a traveler reaches their destination after following the roadmap, the heroes reach their reward at the end of their journey.

The hero's journey is a tried-and-true formula that has been used successfully for thousands of years to tell captivating stories and you can successfully use it in your business. Some of the highlights of the chapter were what is the hero's journey, how to use the hero's journey in business, and how to write a great hero's journey story.

By correctly applying the hero's journey, storytellers can create stories that are engaging and relatable, tapping into universal themes and emotions. The hero's journey provides a framework for telling stories that are inspiring, memorable, and meaningful.

The next chapter is fundamentally important as we will be talking about the NBA Storytelling Technique, a key framework that is highly enshrined in this five-part storytelling series.

CHAPTER 6: NBA STORYTELLING TECHNIQUE

Imagine a story that doesn't merely unfold but dances before your eyes, a narrative that doesn't just recount events but immerses you in them. This is the magic of the N.B.A. storytelling technique.

The N.B.A. technique isn't just another storytelling formula; it's a revelation of how our human experience is inherently woven into the fabric of time. It breaks away from the confines of chronological order and takes you on a ride through the power of Now, Before, and After.

The N.B.A. principles are designed as the compass to guide you through this five-part book storytelling series. And that is well thought out. Are you ready for the ride? Then let's get started.

Welcome to chapter 6 of the book, Storytelling Basics: How To Get Started In Telling Impactful Stories. This is an essential chapter of the book, where we will learn about the storytelling technique that runs across, not only this book but the entire five-part book series.

By the end of this chapter, you should understand what is meant by The N.B.A. storytelling technique, what is the idea behind the technique such as the philosophical thoughts that "Before anything, there was something else" and some practical application of the technique.

You will also understand the effectiveness of the N.B.A. storytelling techniques and how to apply them in a sales story and more.

The N.B.A. technique

The N.B.A. storytelling technique, which stands for Now, Before, and After provides a clear framework for good narrative flow of storytelling.

The technique is based on the principle that effective storytelling involves establishing a strong connection with the audience, immersing them in the narrative, and building anticipation for what is to come.

By dividing the story into three distinct parts – "Now, Before, and After", this technique enables storytellers to engage their audience at various levels, keeping them emotionally invested and curious throughout the journey.

Unlike the regular chronological order of events as the past, the present, and the future, the N.B.A technique starts at the current moment or event, back into the future for the cause of the event, and then looks towards the future after the event so we can better understand the consequences of what has happened.

This is because we are always in the present (now), which is what we are more aware of than any other time frame. We know we came from somewhere (before), the history of how we got to the present and of course the future (after) which is what happens after now.

Now, let's clarify a bit more for better understanding. This might be a little too philosophical for some, but we need a better understanding of the NBA principles as that will guide us throughout what remains of the five-part book series.

Before anything, there was something else

Let us begin our journey by looking at the natural world. Consider the life-giving rain that falls from the sky (Now). (Before) each drop descends, it arises from the vast oceans, lakes, and rivers of our planet.

These bodies of water have their own intricate histories, shaped by the ebb and flow of time. In essence, before the raindrop, there was water, and before the water, there were geological processes, evaporation, and condensation. Each drop was a brief but beautiful manifestation, which resulted from a long chain of "something else."

Life itself follows a similar pattern. Think about a seed sprouting into a mighty tree (Now). (Before) the majestic oak, there was the seed, cradled in the soil, absorbing nutrients and energy from the Earth and the sun.

This transformation from a tiny seed to a towering tree is a testament to the idea that before the tree, there was the seed, and before the seed, there was the complex dance of life, with countless species interwoven in an intricate ecological web. I sincerely hope you are getting the picture.

You see, in human society, we find further evidence of this principle. Consider the invention of the internet, a vast digital network connecting people across the globe. (Before) the internet, there were computers, and before computers, there were mathematical theories, electrical engineering breakthroughs, and the desire for seamless communication.

The internet, though might remain a marvel of modern society, emerged from a series of innovations, each building upon something else that came before it.

This philosophical idea can also be applied to our common understanding of knowledge itself. Before we can comprehend new ideas (Now), we must first have a foundation of existing knowledge.

Every discovery, every scientific breakthrough, and every artistic masterpiece is built upon the accumulated wisdom of previous generations. Before the new, there is the old, serving as the steppingstone for the progress we see around us including the possible future.

In essence, the notion that "before anything, there was something else" is about the interconnectedness of existence. It underscores the idea that nothing emerges in isolation but is always part of an ongoing and ever-evolving narrative.

You would have noticed that in explaining the idea that before anything, there was something else, I didn't even mention the last component of the NBA which is the after. Well, that is where the interpretation of and the creativity of the storyteller comes into play.

Based on the reason or objective of your storytelling, you can project the future and therefore the (After). Now, let's talk about how to apply the NBA storytelling technique in a more practical sense.

Practical application of the technique:

> ### *Now – the current situation*

Imagine (now) as the present moment of the story. Whether you are looking at your business pitch to investors, proposing a change to a community situation, or speaking to a group of army generals to rally their troops around for war, the layout is going to be about the same.

Start by introducing a captivating scene or a significant event that grabs the audience's attention immediately. This helps you to set the stage by describing the current situation, highlighting the main characters, and providing essential context.

The "Now" phase serves as the anchor point for the story and should create a sense of immediacy and relevance to the current time and situation.

> ### *Before – what happened before now.*

Once the audience is hooked, transition into the "Before" phase. Remember that before anything, there was something else. So, take a step back in time to provide backstory, context, and character development. By exploring the events that led up to the current situation, you will deepen the audience's understanding of the characters and their motivations.

Do not underestimate this because people always attach themselves to the stories and events of the past. So, follow this natural pattern and you will never need to struggle so hard to take them along in your narratives.

Note that this section helps to build emotional connections and investment in the story. And like I was saying before, this is fundamental as it shows what had happened before now.

> ### After – the consequence of what has happened

After thoroughly exploring the "Before" phase, move into the "After" phase. This is where the consequences, resolutions, or outcomes of the story unfold. It can involve resolving conflicts, revealing the aftermath of events, or presenting the transformation of characters.

The "After" phase should also provide closure and satisfaction to the audience while leaving room for reflection or anticipation.

By employing the N.B.A. storytelling technique, you can create a dynamic and engaging narrative structure that keeps the audience hooked throughout. It allows you to strategically reveal information, maintain suspense, and build emotional connections.

Now, here are some additional tips to make the technique even more effective in your storytelling:

- Maintain a balance between the three phases, ensuring that each receives adequate attention while maintaining continuity.
- Use cliffhangers or unexpected twists to transition between the different phases, leaving the audience eager for more.
- Experiment with the order of the phases to create variations in storytelling, depending on the desired impact.
- Pay attention to pacing, ensuring a smooth flow between the phases to avoid jarring transitions.
- Remember to incorporate sensory details, emotions, and vivid descriptions to immerse the audience in the story and enhance their engagement.
- By applying the N.B.A. storytelling technique, you can craft compelling narratives that captivate your audience, build anticipation, and leave a lasting impression.

Now you might be thinking: are there some examples out there where this technique has been used before? Well, the answer is yes, and here are three good examples of the NBA technique from popular films. Pay attention to the usage:

➤ *"Inception" (2010):*

- **Now**: The film starts with a captivating scene where Dom Cobb (Leonardo DiCaprio) wakes up on a beach and appears disoriented. The immediate sense of urgency and confusion grabs the audience's attention. "What is going on?", they wondered, and you probably did too if you were seeing the film for the first time.
- **Before**: As the story progresses, the film delves into Cobb's backstory, exploring his past experiences with dream manipulation and his personal struggles. This phase provides context and emotional depth to his character. This helps the audience to understand what has happened before.
- **After**: The film builds towards the resolution, where the consequences of Cobb's actions in the dream world are revealed. The "After" phase involves a climactic sequence that determines the fate of the characters and leaves the audience with a thought-provoking ending. You are not sure you got that? Well, let's check out another example.

➤ *"Pulp Fiction" (1994):*

- **Now**: The film opens with a tense scene where Vincent Vega (John Travolta) and

Jules Winnfield (Samuel L. Jackson) discuss the meaning of a foot massage. The dialogue-driven scene immediately immerses the audience in the story. But what does that mean and where are the characters coming from?

- **Before**: Through a series of nonlinear narratives, the film explores the backstories of various characters, providing context and establishing connections between their lives. Yes, something had happened before. This phase in the story adds depth to the characters and builds anticipation in the audience.

- **After**: The "After" phase involves the resolution of multiple storylines and the consequences of the characters' actions. The film presents unexpected twists, creating a sense of satisfaction and reflection for the audience. Now, below is another example, so you can get a full understanding of what I am talking about.

➤ *"The Social Network" (2010):*

- **Now**: The film opens with Mark Zuckerberg (Jesse Eisenberg) in a heated conversation with his girlfriend, foreshadowing the conflicts to come. The immediate tension draws the audience into the story. But that is not where it all started.

- **Before**: The film delves into the events leading up to the creation of Facebook, exploring Zuckerberg's motivations, relationships, and the challenges he faces. This phase provides insight into his character and the origins of the social media platform.

- **After**: The "After" phase focuses on the aftermath of Zuckerberg's actions, including legal battles and the impact of Facebook's success. It showcases the consequences of his choices and leaves the audience with a sense of reflection on the power and consequences of social media.

These examples demonstrate how the N.B.A. storytelling techniques can be applied in different ways to engage the audience, build emotional connections, and create a cohesive narrative structure.

Of course, your stories are most certainly going to be different from the examples above, but you can always apply the technique, remembering that before anything, there is always something else.

Build your audience's anticipation by helping them to understand the current situation, and take them behind to the backstory so they can fully appreciate what led to the present state of things. Satisfy their curiosity by forging a new meaning after what happened before.

The effectiveness of the N.B.A. storytelling techniques

The N.B.A. (Now, Before, and After) storytelling technique is highly effective for several reasons and can be considered a superior approach to storytelling for various purposes. Here's an explanation of its effectiveness and why it's a valuable storytelling method:

1. **Engages the Audience:** The N.B.A. technique immediately draws the audience into the narrative by starting with the "Now" phase, which represents the current situation or the main events. This engages the audience's attention and curiosity from the outset, making them eager to learn more about what's happening.

2. **Provides Context:** By including the "Before" phase, this technique offers essential context and background information. Context is critical for the audience to fully understand the significance of the events unfolding in the "Now" phase. It also answers the "why" behind the story, making it more relatable and meaningful.

3. **Highlights Cause and Effect:** The N.B.A. technique excels at showing cause-and-effect relationships. It demonstrates how past events or decisions in the "Before" phase led to the current situation in the "Now" phase. This makes the story more logical and helps the audience connect the dots more easily.

4. **Builds Suspense and Tension:** The structured progression from "Now" to "Before" creates a natural sense of suspense and tension. The audience is initially presented with a problem or situation and then taken back in time to explore its origins. This format keeps them engaged and eager to uncover what led to the current scenario.

5. **Supports Character Development:** In stories involving characters, the N.B.A. technique allows for effective character development. It lets you introduce characters in the "Before" phase, showcasing their motivations, personalities, and struggles, and then follow their evolution through the "Now" phase. This depth makes the characters more relatable and compelling.

6. **Offers Resolution and Closure:** Finally, the "After" phase provides resolution and closure to the story. It allows the audience

to see the outcomes of the events in the "Now" phase and reflect on the journey. This helps create a satisfying and memorable storytelling experience.

7. **Adaptable and Versatile:** The N.B.A. technique is versatile and adaptable to various storytelling contexts. Whether you are crafting a personal narrative, business presentation, historical account, or fictional story, this method can be applied to convey your message effectively.

8. **Enhances Message Retention:** Because the N.B.A. technique presents information in a structured and logical sequence, it enhances message retention. Audiences are more likely to remember and understand the key points of the story when it follows a clear structure.

In summary, the N.B.A. storytelling technique is effective because it engages the audience and provides context. It equally helps to highlight cause and effect, builds suspense, supports character development, and it's easily adaptable to different storytelling contexts.

How the NBA storytelling technique can be applied in a sales story

The N.B.A. (Now, Before, and After) storytelling technique can be highly effective in a sales story to engage potential customers, communicate the value of your product or service, and ultimately drive conversions. Here is how you can apply the N.B.A. technique in a sales story, in three steps each:

> *Now:*

1. **Set the Scene:** Begin your sales story in the present moment. Introduce the audience to the current challenges, pain points, or needs that your potential customers are facing. Create a relatable scenario that resonates with them.

2. **Problem Identification:** Clearly identify and emphasize the problem or challenge your product or service is designed to solve. This should be a problem that your audience can relate to and is actively seeking a solution to. Use data, anecdotes, or customer testimonials to validate the issue.

3. **Engage and Connect:** Connect with your audience on an emotional level by highlighting the frustration, inconvenience, or dissatisfaction associated with the current situation. Make them feel that you understand their pain and are empathetic to their needs.

➢ *Before:*

1. **Transition to the Past:** Shift the narrative to the "Before" phase, which represents the situation before your product or service came into the picture. Describe the difficulties, limitations, or inefficiencies that your potential customers experienced in the absence of your solution. That is also the time to look at the possible cause of a problem or how the client got to the current situation.

2. **Highlight the Gap:** Illustrate the stark contrast between the problems identified in the "Now" phase and the challenges faced by individuals or businesses in the "Before" phase. Clearly articulate the gap between their current situation and their desired outcome.

3. **Build Tension:** Create a sense of anticipation and tension by showcasing the obstacles and frustrations that your potential customers encountered as they tried to address the problem without your product or service. Use good storytelling techniques to make this phase relatable and engaging.

➢ *After:*

1. **Introduce Your Solution:** Finally, transition to the "After" phase, where you present your product or service as the solution to the problems and challenges outlined in the previous phases. Explain how your offering addresses their pain points and provides a clear path to achieving their desired outcomes. At this phase, the clients need to know what will happen after applying your solution.

2. **Benefits and Transformations:** Highlight the specific benefits and transformations that customers can expect to experience by using your product or service. Share success stories, case studies, or real-world examples that demonstrate how others have benefited from your solution.

3. **Outcome Visualization:** Paint a vivid picture of what life looks like after your product or service has been adopted. Help your audience imagine the positive changes, increased efficiency, or improved results they will enjoy by choosing your solution.

4. **Call to Action:** Conclude with a compelling call to action that encourages your audience to take the next step, whether it's making a purchase, requesting

a demo, or contacting your sales team. Clearly communicate the value of acting now and the potential consequences of inaction.

I believe you now get the full picture. By applying the N.B.A. storytelling technique in a sales story, you can create a narrative that resonates with your audience, establishes the need for your product or service, and motivates them to act.

This structured approach can help you communicate your value proposition effectively and engage potential customers on both an emotional and rational level.

Storytelling guide – NBA storytelling technique

The NBA storytelling technique, if well executed, is a powerful narrative structure that can be used in various forms of storytelling, including literature, film, marketing, and public speaking.

The technique involves presenting a story or information in three distinct parts as "Now" "Before" and "After". Do you want to get more out of your narratives, using the NBA storytelling technique? Then pay attention to the following guides:

1. **Engagement:** Make sure your story is engaging. Starting with the "Now" will help you capture your audience's attention and immediately, make them interested in what's happening at that moment. This engagement is crucial for keeping your audience invested in the narrative.
2. **Clarity:** Use the "Before" section to provide context and background information, which is essential for understanding the current situation. It will help to prevent confusion and ensure that the audience has the necessary information to follow the story or the message you are passing across.
3. **Anticipation:** You can use the "After" phase to create anticipation and suspense. Do this to keep the audience curious about what will happen next, encouraging them to stay engaged and invested in the story or message until the end.
4. **Emotional Connection:** By moving through the stages of "Now," "Before," and "After," you can evoke a range of emotions in your audience. They can empathize with the characters or the situation, as they understand the context and anticipate the potential outcomes.

Your takeaway from Chapter Six

This chapter of the book is essential not only to this book but to the entire five-part book series. It laid the foundation for the storytelling technique we will refer to several times in this book.

During the chapter, we considered what it meant by the NBA storytelling technique before exploring some philosophical thought that before anything, there was something else. That was an important consideration.

We equally talked about some practical applications before looking at the effectiveness of the storytelling techniques and how they can be applied in a sales story. You don't want to underestimate that, especially if you are interested in business storytelling which I think you should.

In essence, the NBA storytelling technique is valuable because it engages the audience, provides context, and helps convey information more effectively. It's a versatile tool for storytellers, communicators, and marketers to better engage and connect with their audience. That is an important takeaway from this chapter of the book.

CONCLUSION

Congratulations and thank you for reading to the end of this book, 'Storytelling Basics: How To Get Started In Telling Impactful Stories'.

The book provides valuable insights and practical advice for small business owners and content creators who are looking for ways to improve their storytelling skills so they can earn more.

Through its clear and concise guidance, this book empowers its readers to turn their ideas into compelling narratives that engage and inspire their audiences.

Whether you are a seasoned content creator or just starting out, what you have gained in this book is a comprehensive introduction to the art of storytelling. You need this knowledge so you can benefit more from the other books that will follow in the series.

Let me repeat that storytelling is an art form that has been around since the beginning of human history.

Whether you are interested in oral storytelling, writing short stories, or creating compelling narratives for film or theatre, getting started in storytelling requires a basic understanding of the elements that make up a good story. You, sure, need to understand such fundamentals as:

- The story theme,
- The plots,
- The structure,
- And how to organize your story for maximum efficiency.

These are the topics that were exhaustively dealt with in this book as the basics of storytelling.

As was repeatedly stressed in the book, it's important to have a clear understanding of your audience, so you can better tailor your storytelling to their interests and needs. And those elements as well-developed characters and vivid descriptions are going to be required to execute better in your storytelling.

Yes, it requires practice and persistence on your part. With these qualities, anyone can learn the basics of storytelling and develop the skills necessary to create enchanting stories that captivate and inspire others.

So, if you have a passion for storytelling, now is the time to get started and unleash your imagination on the world.

ABOUT THE AUTHOR

My name is Obehi Ewanfoh. I am originally from Nigeria, and I live in Verona, Italy with my family. I am a full-time content creator and I love to create valuable content to inform and educate my audience.

I am the host of the Obehi Podcast where we strongly believe that everyone has a story to share. By everyone, I mean everyone and that includes you.

Upon arriving in Italy in August of 2004, I found myself asking such questions as:

- Who were the first Africans in the city of Verona where I have lived since then?
- What have been their experiences away from their homeland?
- As an immigrant, new to the Northern Italy city of Verona, how could I learn from them?

I could not find any book to read and some of the information I could find here and there was not satisfactory to me, so I decided to start asking more questions and talking to different people with the idea of writing the first book of the African experience in the city.

The research would take more than five years and result in more than two books (*The Journey—Africans In Verona* and *The Color Of Our Children*), in addition to some video documentaries, which were screened in different schools and cultural centers across Northern Italy.

Even then I was still not fully satisfied because there were no real solutions to the complains I heard from people for more than five years, and I was not sure if I had made any real contributions by asking those questions.

A little later, exactly on April the 7th 2019, it occurred to me like a deeper message. I was hospitalized then and I was thinking a lot about this project I have been working on for a long time.

This was when I realized that I really needed to do this. Thinking back to when I was much younger in my hometown of Uromi, Nigeria, and the different books I have written, both published and unpublished.

It came to make sense to me, then, that I was searching for myself, my way of contributing to other people and living a life that truly makes sense to me.

I have since come to appreciate this opportunity of service, of helping other people to find what they truly love and to make their contributions, especially through storytelling and content creation.

Storytelling, you will understand in this book on Storytelling Basics, is a powerful instrument to leverage either for personal use or business purposes. This is why "**The Storytelling Mastery**" was created. It is designed to help you leverage the power of storytelling so you can stand out from the crowd and earn more.

My ultimate mission, through content creation, is to help people, particularly those within the African diaspora community, to transform their human potential into capital so they can better serve themselves and the society they live in.

If you found any value in this book, then it means my journey has somehow been a success. Thank you again for reading, and make sure you check out book two in the series "Win Hearts & Minds and Get Results With The 5 Essential Elements Of Storytelling."

Obehi Ewanfoh

www.ingramcontent.com/pod-product-compliance
Lightning Source LLC
Chambersburg PA
CBHW070554220526
45467CB00003B/1205